MW01110300

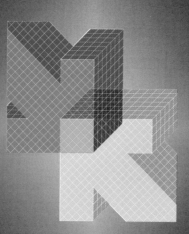

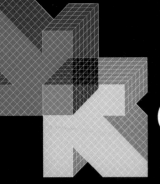

Growth in the Fast Lane

Mergers represent unconventional growth, and that calls for some unconventional moves. Much of what's needed now is counter-intuitive stuff. Status quo management just won't cut it.

Growth in the fast lane requires quicker reflexes. A keener sense of timing. More nerve.

Mergers make things happen in a hurry—you have much more to manage all at once. If you put the company in this particular groove, plan to speed up.

Fast growth calls for fast management.

Of course, this is out of character for many managers and executives. Over the years our corporate world made people more security-oriented... inclined to minimize risks...fond of stability.

That's a slow-growth management style, one that's downright dangerous when you're driving an organization in the fast lane. It does all sorts of damage to the company, and it can wreck careers. It also helps explain why far too many mergers end up in the failure statistics.

For now, you need to *manage more entrepreneurially*, making the moves needed to grow a business rapidly.

Become a scrambler. Accept a work situation with more ragged edges. Make friends with risk. And in spite of all the commotion, concentrate on the essentials: *Think few.*

You're managing in a less forgiving situation for now. You need focus. Concentration. Plus a good dose of determination. The fast lane is a high risk/high reward proposition. You win big, or you lose big.

Just remember—growth has rules. This field manual gives you a powerful set of guidelines to go by as you manage growth through mergers.

PRITCHETT & ASSOCIATES, INC.
Dallas, Texas

TABLE OF CONTENTS

New Game, New Goals
A DECADE OF DIFFERENCE
Mergers Redefined

	Yesterday	*Today*
Reasons	Financial Play	Performance Jump
Risks	Over-leverage	Assimilation/Integration
Targets	Diverse	Similar
Prizes	Tangibles (Plants, Equipment, Inventory, etc.)	Intangibles (Core Competency, Customers, Channels, Content)
Success Factors	Transactional	Operational
Pressure Points	Sequential & Staggered	Parallel & Overlapping
Assets	Financial (Hard Capital)	Intellectual (Soft Capital)
Info. Technology	Centralized	Decentralized
Organization	Functional	Process-driven
Supply	Shortages	Over-capacity
Mandate	Stabilize	Exploit Instability
Market	Forgiving	Merciless

New moves in merger integration strategy.

I n today's business world the game is growth. Ramping up. Getting bigger to get better.

Some companies go at it conservatively, in incremental fashion. Other outfits shoot the works. Their game plan aims at exponential growth, and that usually means mergers and acquisitions...growing by leaps and bounds...combining operations to get maximum market share, economies of scale, payback on technology investments. In other words, major *upsizing*, in high gear.

What's driving this big shift toward dominating instead of downsizing?

Well, it's that same old one syllable word: change. But instead of struggling to cope with change, companies now are trying to conquer it. Today's focus is on building. Buying. And because the world's new, faster metabolism is catching hold, mergers are back.

Sure, shrinking and trimming will continue. We still need to squeeze out costs and soup up performance. But everybody's doing that. And most folks have figured out that cutbacks, by themselves, won't make you competitive for long. Having done some serious pruning, the corporate world now needs a good growing season.

Today's Deals are Different.

The last merger wave, to a large extent, was made up of "financial plays." Today's deals, to a much larger degree, depend on good integration management.

The new game mandates operational effectiveness. So growth via mergers and acquisitions becomes a winning proposition only if the companies can be consolidated successfully. And only if the whole truly is greater than the sum of the parts. Or faster. Or cheaper. Or reaches more customers.

Financial gains are still the final target, of course, but they aren't achieved when the deal is cut. Unlike in times past, today's acquirers don't simply strip away assets and maximize shareholder value in short order. Current mergers are looked at as longer term challenges.

Another difference—yesterday's corporate marriages involved more diverse companies. Acquirers more frequently bought into different industries. Sometimes this was done to smooth out cyclical bumps, to diversify, the hope being that it would hedge an investment portfolio. Companies bought what they didn't know. And what you don't know, they learned, can kill you.

Subsequently, divestiture became the key word, but *garage sale* was more like it. A study of 33 major companies' acquisition activities covering a 36-year span found that over 50 percent of their unrelated acquisitions were later divested.

Today's trend is to acquire companies in the same business, or close to it. Firms that complement, that strengthen your capacity to serve customers. Companies vertically or horizontally related. Sometimes your fiercest competitors...or suppliers...even your customers.

But the risk is still there.

Research shows that related firms are sometimes even harder to assimilate. Why? The acquirer thinks it understands the other business, but often doesn't. Or maybe both companies have the same types of people with similar skills, and that means redundancy. This is the dark side of synergy.

Soft Stuff is Harder to Merge.

These days acquirers aren't necessarily hungry for the target companies' plants, equipment and other hard assets. Now they're going

3

after entirely different prizes. The new aiming points are a company's core competencies. Its customers. Its distribution channels. Its content.

The hot prizes aren't *things*—they're thoughts, methodologies, people and relationships. Soft goods, so to speak.

Look at how many companies are being bought for their patents, licenses, market share, name brand, research staffs, methods, customer base, or culture. IBM didn't buy Lotus for its office buildings, furniture or cash in the bank. It craved Lotus' software development teams, proprietary systems, customer loyalty and such.

And here's the scary part. Soft capital, like this, is very perishable. Very fragile and fluid. Unlike machinery, real estate, inventory and other tangibles, you can't lock it up at night. Nor can you sell it to someone else if it somehow gets away from you.

So you've got to nurture these soft assets. You must seduce them into the new combined enterprise with great care. Then protect them. This takes tremendous skill and finesse.

Consolidating Has Become More Complicated.

Merging never has been a simple drill, but it used to be more straightforward. Slam two departments together, for example, or combine functions. But with all the decentralization that's occurred in the past decade, consolidation of operations isn't so matter-of-fact.

Consider what's happened to our information systems (IS). They've gone from glass houses with mainframes and an hierarchical organization, to far-flung networks run on a shared basis. Pulling these multiple IS capabilities together is like herding cats. Some of what we're integrating lives in cyberspace. And some travels at the speed of light. Hard to find, hard to catch, hard to consolidate.

Of course, we've atomized more than IS. We've knocked out layers of management and spread responsibility all around. We've torn down functional stovepipes. We've reengineered work into processes rather than discrete tasks.

And this brings up a key point.

As many companies invested heavily in business process reengineering, functional groups were disbanded or bypassed. Work got redefined and redistributed. People were given wider ranges of responsibility. New work teams were formed, and some were given very general authority to plan and conduct work. We broke organizations apart and formed them into new patterns.

So far so good. But now along comes a merger.

Can Reengineering Survive a Merger?

The integration process puts reengineering to a new test: How easily can two reengineered companies consolidate? What if one is process-driven and the other is still structured by function? What if one works on a geographic basis and the other by product line? What if one has reengineered extensively while the other is just beginning?

Merging two stand-alone *purchasing departments*, for example, is complicated enough. How does one merge two highly integrated *value chains*, each deeply intertwined with suppliers, contractors and customers?

The classic divisions that once ruled organizations are fading fast. Many executives and managers have been involved in merging functional organizations, but how many have consolidated reengineered ones? Very few people have the know-how needed to put the new mosaic together.

It's pioneering. And pioneering has a high failure rate.

On top of all this, today's mergers are being played out among a more jaded, change-fatigued work force. They're occurring in markets where customers have more purchase options than ever. Amidst a global set of competitors. In a dizzying parade of technological advances.

This means you must contend with more pressure points than ever before.

Been There? Done That?

Mergers always have pushed people's change management skills to the limit. Now they're pushing even harder.

To pull this off successfully—to win at the fast growth game of mergers—you need to follow some new rules. The mere fact that you've played the game in years past should not make you rest easily with today's merger challenges. It's a different game these days, and you can't afford to confuse *experience* with *expertise*.

The following pages frame out a fresh set of guidelines. Weave these into your integration strategy, and make yourself a winner in the new game of growth.

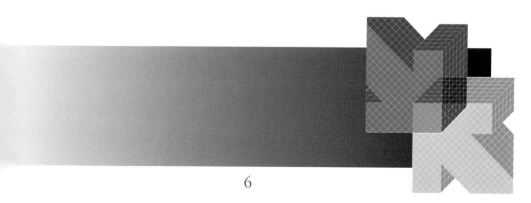

Burn up the road.

W'll start with a one-question quiz: What do you think is the single best predictor of successful merger integration?

And here's the answer: The length of the transition period.

The longer you take to integrate, the closer you live to the edge. Disappointing deals correlate highly with slow consolidation.

Decades of merger experience prove this. The turtle may win the race in fairy tales, but not in the grinding, gut-wrenching, high risk game of merger integration. We've been saying this for years, and it's coming close to being accepted now as conventional wisdom. Here's the problem— companies still demonstrate big differences of opinion regarding what "fast" really is.

Some organizations, we all know, are notoriously slow. They can speed up significantly, and still be dragging their feet to a dangerous degree. Who comes to mind? Utilities. Some insurance companies. Governmental agencies. Not-for-profit organizations. And some of America's corporate giants that lumber along like cargo planes in a competitive world better suited for fighter jets.

In fact, even those companies that could consider themselves respectably fast in the way they merged during the '80s may be sluggish by today's standards.

Most mergers are still taking much longer than they should. Sure, companies are picking up the pace, but the world of change is accelerating even faster. So before they finish the consolidation, they get hit by other changes that demand management's attention and that suck up financial resources. The more leisurely you proceed with the merger integration process, the more you're likely to end up a victim of change overload.

We still see executives—highly capable business people—who sit down, reason among themselves, and conclude that, by golly, they're going to take the time needed to do it *right*. Sounds good in theory, fails miserably in practice. When it comes to speed of execution, so-called "prudence" shapes up as a reckless strategy. You'll hear people argue that they need to study the situation a little longer, weigh the alternatives one more time, consider all the angles, wait until they get everybody on board.

Our recommendation? Don't give in to that garbage.

You are in a race. A race against the operating problems that are just generic to mergers. A race against competitors who are building counter-strategies. A race against employee complacency. And a race against your critics—the resisters, nay-sayers, and negative-minded people who would love to see you fail. You just can't afford to tolerate any form of procrastination, even when it masquerades as prudence. While you pause, your competitors push ahead. While you ponder, your customers will abandon you. Decide to deliberate a little longer, and you'll let the resisters gain the upper ground.

It's essential, then, that you combat the natural tendency to study the situation and try to craft the perfect integration plan. There are no perfect solutions in the new game of mergers. Only good and timely ones.

So exploit the speed advantage. Use it to implement solutions before your critics can even isolate the problems. Use it to disorient those clinging to the status quo. Now's the time for a fastbreak offense, for instant momentum. Speed—*real speed*—stacks the odds in your favor.

Engineer some early wins.

E very merger, once announced, is immediately put on trial. Top management—those who crafted the deal—also stand accused. And the accusers just keep crawling out of the woodwork as several months go by.

Often word of the merger leaks out during the negotiation stage, and the criticism cranks up before the deal is even done. Otherwise, top management gets to tell its story first. This is a crucial opportunity, but far too often executives blow their chances at properly setting the stage for what's to come. They also say things that are guaranteed to come back to haunt them. Besides all that, however, talk is cheap. Top officials can carry on all day about how great the merger is going to be. They can praise its potential, and promise people the moon. But there are many disbelievers.

The press hovers close by, hoping to report something provocative and controversial. They like bad news the best. Also, the investment community may have a sour attitude. The competition is always chomping at the bit, looking for trouble they can talk about to your customers. As for the employee audience, well, they're listening with a lot of skepticism, suspicion, hostility and fear.

This is a hard-nosed jury here. To a large extent, top management and the merger are guilty until proven innocent. And now for the worst part of it all: the critics get their proof first.

Think about it. A merger is a very strategic move. But early on, there are many tactical problems. You don't do a merger because it brings you an immediate high, or because you get instant payoff. For the most part, the good stuff takes quite a while to materialize. This is a prime example of "deferred gratification," where the organization decides to go through the difficult drill of merging for the eventual benefits it will bring.

Meanwhile, the critics have a field day, calling attention to the generic merger problems as proof that the merger was ill-conceived or is being poorly executed. Their evidence? Sagging morale. A weakening trust level across the organization. Erosion of job commitment. Power struggles and turf battles. High stress. Loss of company loyalty. Confusion and frustration. Finally, and probably most important, a downturn in productivity.

Now if they really knew what they were talking about—and if they wanted to play fair—they would admit that this is a completely normal turn of events. It goes with the territory. These problems just prove a merger is going on, not whether it's good or bad.

It may strike you as perverse, but, frankly, you should be very vocal in predicting these problems. Better to come across as a wise prophet and prepare your employees for the problems that are bound to come, rather than leave the anti-change crowd free to exploit the situation to its advantage.

Still, telling people what to expect is not nearly enough. You need quick accomplishments you can celebrate publicly. To offset the scorn and suspicion, you need some rapid success. Somehow you need to protect the deal by developing hard proof that things are headed in the right direction.

So what do early wins look like?

- The two company leaders have met and get along. *("They're real people!")*
- A new name and logo are rolled out. *("It's pretty snappy.")*
- Employee benefits packages are consolidated. *("We're not forgotten.")*
- A big sale is completed. *("We can work together.")*
- Deserving candidates are promoted. *("There's room for winners here.")*
- Unpopular product lines are killed off. *("It's about time.")*
- One company adopts the other's best practices. *("We can learn from them.")*
- Onerous policies and procedures are discontinued. *("Finally!")*

Far more convincing than all that, though, are *financial victories.* As the saying goes, money doesn't talk, it screams.

When the numbers stack up favorably, people pay attention. If you can show quick merger payoffs that carry dollar signs, the gripers, whiners, and other nay-sayers start losing credibility and resistance starts to soften.

Communicate at E-speed.

Word flies as soon as people pick up the scent that a merger is in the works. This is high drama. Hot stuff. Everybody has an opinion, and all the rules of gossip prevail. For the next several months you're fighting a war for the truth.

Nothing new about that. What *is* different these days, though, is the way word travels. In just a few short years, communication has developed a far greater range (worldwide), more rapid cruising speed (fast as light), and accessibility to all (the "wired world").

Today messages crisscross the planet at E-speed. The lowest employee in your organization can hit the Internet, tune in to the World Wide Web, or simply shoot word instantly to others via E-mail, fax, cellular phone or voice mail. In the past you worried about the grapevine and tried to control the rumor mill. Today that means controlling the light waves, the electron stream. You just can't contain information like you did. Neither can you wait a week or so to respond to questions, concerns, suppositions or false stories.

Remember, a merger is always a fast-breaking story. Every day brings new developments. The truth is a moving target, and often dead on arrival. In your efforts to control communications and manage messages, you're not going to get by with an 800 number or a company newsletter that comes out once a month or even every week. You need a home page on the Net. An E-mail burst. Chat rooms. Videoconferencing. A barrage of rumors reverberates through the wired world, from legitimate and other sources. You've got to get your message through. At E-speed. And it had better be tight, sound and consistent. Otherwise, the critics will electrocute it.

We're living in a networked world these days, and you need to take the high ground in cyberspace as well as with conventional communication channels. Your job? Get there first—to listen, and to feed a steady stream of honest, positive, proactive messages to all key stakeholders. In fact, today's mergers need a communication manager, an "information czar," a dedicated person serving as message central for merger news.

Your ambition should be to over-communicate. Don't worry about redundancy here, or that people will resent being told twice or tire of the message. Never suppose the obvious is apparent to others. There is no penalty for talking too much.

Silence, on the other hand, is a major sin. It creates an information vacuum, and that's something mergers abhor. If you're not filling the communication void, somebody will—with rumors, fearmongering, wishful thinking, warped information, and even outright lies. Plus, with modern technology readily at hand, anybody who really wants to can stir up trouble by communicating faster, easier, and to more people than was ever possible before.

Two-way communications are critical for the foreseeable future. So first, magnetize yourself to bad news. You want it coming to you rather than going to others. If you know what the problems are, chances are you can fix them. Make it easy for people to communicate what's going wrong, and never shoot the messengers. And again, be overly generous with outbound information. Become a perpetual communications machine—e.g., talk too much, write too much, explain too frequently, listen excessively. In times of great uncertainty, this is how you learn and how you lead.

In the process of keeping all your people updated, tell *why* before how or what. Today's "thought workers" want more than mere orders. They want reasons...logic...rationale. They'll accept just about anything so long as it makes sense to them, no matter how difficult or disappointing. Articulate the logic behind the merger, and they'll help you create the *how* to make it work.

Just one final note: Don't blow smoke. Don't shave the truth. Don't play the propaganda game. You can't con these people, at least not for long. Besides, you're dealing with adults here, and they deserve the truth. Build your credibility by leveling with them. Give it to them straight—the good, the bad and the ugly. Arm them with understanding—feed them a steady flow of accurate information—if you want to enlist their support for the merger.

Push through the yield point.

Opposition surfaces as soon as the integration process gets underway. Resistance starts to climb. You push to change the organization, and it starts pushing back. People gripe, whine and criticize, complaining about your objectives as well as the way in which you're trying to reach them. Pretty soon the noise level begins to hurt your ears.

Under ordinary circumstances, negative reactions this strong mean you're doing something wrong. In the merger scenario, though, they more likely mean you're doing things dead right.

Still, resistance gets your attention. And the stronger the reaction of the anti-change crowd, the more you're inclined to question your goals or methodologies. Challenged by others, you begin to challenge yourself. Whispers of doubt start circulating in your head. Part of you says, "Don't push so hard...Take it easy...The organization has had all it can take—better back off, regroup, let things settle down a little."

These are signals that you're approaching a super-critical junction in the merger integration process. You're coming up on what we call the *yield point*, one of the make-or-break stages en route to merger success. The organization had to struggle to get here. Now it's gut check time. The resisters are saying, "We can't (or won't) take any more!" What you need to know is that you're on the threshold of something big. You're not on the verge of *breakdown*, you're poised for *breakthrough*.

Everything you've done up to this point is on the line. You've paid your dues, and you're just one step away from payoff. You're about to gain quantum advantage.

But if you quit now, you get nothing. Lose your resolve before passing through the yield point, and it has all been wasted effort.

Actually, yield point is a term from the vocabulary of physics. Scientists test materials this way. They apply pressure and measure the stretching it produces. For example, they put a steel bar in a vise and crank up the psi (pounds of pressure per square inch). It stretches until they let off the pressure, and then the bar snaps back to its original size and shape. This range of movement is called the "elastic zone." Once the pressure bends or stretches the metal past a certain point, though, the resistance to change stops. The steel bar has moved beyond the "elastic zone" and no longer snaps back to its original shape. It enters the "plastic zone."

Organizations tend to act that way, too. And in managing mergers, you need to keep the pressure on for change, even increase the pressure, until you hit the yield point. Then, with one more tiny push, the organization moves beyond that crucial threshold and enters the plastic zone. Here, change sticks. There's no going back to the way things were. The resistance disappears.

What we're saying here is that the path to merger success isn't a steady, consistent, incremental process where each effort you make toward integration is matched by parallel gains. In the early stages of consolidation, you put forth a lot of effort but seem to get little accomplished. Then you hit the yield point, and that last little bit of effort gives great rewards. A dime of work buys a dollar's worth of change.

Here's why. Before your organization reaches the yield point, the various merger objectives are seen as possibilities. Maybes. Beyond the yield point, an objective has been realized, and is an absolute, uncontested fact. In the struggle up to the yield point, change is seen as optional. Once you move beyond it to the other side, change is mandatory. The critics cause trouble right up to the yield point. Then they quit fighting you. That particular war is over.

So there you are—hanging on the precipice of failure, and standing on the edge of success. Your move. This is where you face the greatest temptation to give in, to cut your people some slack. It seems like an act of management kindness toward them, and it sure seems easiest for you. Conventional wisdom tells you to relent a little, to rest and gather strength. But softening your stance usually just stiffens the opposition. The resisters will take heart and find new faith in their cause if your determination starts to weaken.

Now's the time to hang tough. To stay the course. Push the organization past the yield point and enter the "plastic zone." The yield point is like the sound barrier—it's turbulent just before you reach it, but smooth as silk once it's broken.

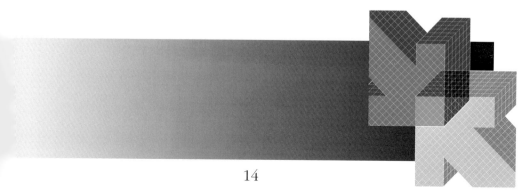

14

Forget about building a common corporate culture.

L et's clear the air on this corporate culture stuff. What it is, whether it's important or not, and what you should do about it for now.

To begin with, corporate culture is something you deal with *indirectly*. Why? Because culture is an intangible. A shadow. A side-effect. You can't grab hold of culture. It has no handles, nothing you can touch directly. In fact, it's a pretty fuzzy concept. And there are a lot of goofy notions surrounding the subject. Having said all that, it is an important issue.

So what should you be doing about corporate culture in the context of today's mergers?

First of all, let's remember that you're a business manager, not an anthropologist. Your big job for now centers around productivity, profits and people. You should keep your eyes trained on achieving hard results, rather than letting your attention wander off into the soft, vague fog of culture. Your job is to fly the jet, not to fool around with its vapor trail. Keep the organization on course...Speed through the integration...Maneuver ahead of the competition. The primary challenges now are *operational* in nature, not *cultural.*

Of course, cultural differences will cause headaches in the process of merging the various parts of the two organizations. We're not denying that. But focusing on operating results does far more to reconcile culture problems than focusing on culture does to deliver the operating results you desperately need.

Our recommendation? Quickly determine the key cultural differences between the specific parts of the two organizations that you, personally, are responsible for helping to merge. Make this a fast, localized evaluation—a side-by-side departmental comparison, for example—not a comprehensive, cross-company study that drags on for months. Get help with this if you need to, just don't let it become a long, drawn out exercise. Get it done early on—should take less than a week.

Then, communicate to your people what the key differences are. Be upfront. Talk in specifics. Take pains to ensure that they follow what you're saying. Next, state clearly any changes that will be made going forward. And explain why you're making these culture shifts. Basically what this simple management act comes down to is this: You're helping them "break the code" quickly, rather than leaving them to wander along for months or years wondering what the prevailing cultural bylaws will be.

Now for this idea of creating a "common" corporate culture, the notion of blending the two different global cultures into one. You know how the party

15

line reads on this, how top executives talk about "taking the best of both worlds," the intent being to build some sort of super-culture. This line of reasoning deserves careful scrutiny. Just how realistic is this now, really, given everything else that's going on? We've got power struggles, turf battles, people jockeying for position. The trust level is in the tank. The rumor mill is running wild. Stress is hitting all time highs. It's the most politically charged climate you'll find anywhere. In the midst of all this, you want to attempt the impossible? Forget it.

Let's be realistic. You can't pull that off right now. Besides, it's a search for fool's gold. If you found it, you wouldn't be able to buy anything with it.

Somehow, over the past decade or so, we've been sold this bill of goods about the need to create a common (shared) culture when two companies merge. But if you look at either organization even before the merger, what you see is primarily a collection of subcultures. Study almost any company, and what you find is a confederation of tribes. Their differences outnumber their similarities.

Look around. Do the people in marketing work in the same ways as those in accounting? Does the legal staff operate with the same intensity, drive, and degree of risk as the sales team? How does upper management behavior look compared to that found in the lower echelons? Compare your Denver people to your folks in Detroit, or the culture of your New York City crowd to that of the small crew in Ponca City, Oklahoma.

Are we saying you should trash the popular concept of corporate culture? Not at all. It's the word "common" that needs dumping.

A few shared values...a couple of operating principles common to all parts of the organization...a small handful of company-wide standards. That's okay. That makes sense. That much you can get across to everybody and try to uphold or enforce.

Beyond that, you should manage the merger toward corporate culture diversity. Toward peaceful coexistence of the many tribes—different people, working in different ways, converging on common goals...*not* conforming to a pervasive corporate culture.

That's reality-based management. You can actually pull that off success-fully. And that cultural mix positions you best to beat the pants off the competition.

Manage expectations.

Mergers can be won or lost before any real integration work ever begins.

As soon as a deal is struck, the battle begins for people's minds. Win that one, and you're well on your way. Lose that fight, and your merger is far more likely to wind up in the failure statistics.

You should move swiftly and purposefully to shape opinions. To set the proper expectations. Insiders and outsiders alike immediately start forming their own ideas about the deal. Some people don't like the looks of it and start lobbying against the merger. Part of your job is to promote it. Defending the merger gets dangerous, though, if you pump people up too much. Setting precisely the right expectations is sort of like threading a needle. Lean a little too far either way, and the job gets harder than it has to be.

First announcements from top management typically put heavy emphasis on the merger's appealing aspects. This is always a sales job, with the maximum amount of positive spin. The risk here is over-promising.

Instead of investing so much mental energy and air time gushing about the "good news," executives would be better off to present a far more balanced viewpoint. All managers, in fact, should be very frank in pointing out the cons as well as the pros.

The media, for its part, ordinarily comes with a more critical eye and more negative stance. These are the folks who thrive on controversy. They'd rather report trouble, because it sells better than good news. So they wag their heads, utter solemn concerns, and call attention to anything they can conjure up that could go wrong. If the deal-makers outdo themselves as merger evangelists, the media people are even better at badmouthing the deal.

No wonder managing expectations is such hard work.

The first ground rule for being good at this is to protect your credibility. After all, you've got to be believable. Without that you can't carry much influence over other people's ideas and opinions. This helps explain why it's important to report both the favorable and not-so-favorable sides of the merger story—people will put more faith in what you say, because it sounds less like propaganda.

During times like these you also need to exercise more "mouth control." In the super-charged atmosphere of a merger, almost anything managers say can be used against them. This is not a matter of saying less. It's about being more careful in what you say, how you say it, and to whom.

So pick your words carefully. Don't presume there has to be a signed contract for people to take what you say as a firm commitment. Like a raw nerve, they react to the slightest hint or innuendo, reading more into your statements than you intend. And just as you're going to have to work harder to manage your mouth, you also have to control your heart. Don't get swept up in the euphoria of a deal or the heat of the moment. You'll say something you'll hate yourself for in the morning.

What's a promise you can't keep? Try these on for size:

- *"This is a win-win situation."* Somewhere, people will feel like they've lost, and they'll say you reneged.

- *"We plan to complete the integration by the end of the next quarter."* Be careful here, because most mergers take about twice as long as expected. Miss one milestone and the critics will howl.

- *"There will be no layoffs, reductions in force, terminations, and so forth."* Let's get serious. Every merger is a financial proposition justified by either cost reductions or revenue enhancements. Quite often, either case calls for streamlining, reengineering, downsizing—if not in the aggregate, at least in pockets of the organization.

- *"We plan to continue business as usual."* If this were true, why merge? A merger is the supreme case of business as unusual.

Another key aspect of managing expectations is to help people understand that the merger integration period is a transitional phase. It's merely a *passage*—a troubled time, yes, but the organization will move beyond these problems. You must clarify that point. Otherwise people will confuse the issue, presuming that the pain of merging is what life will be like after the merger is complete. Help them grasp the fact that this, too, shall pass.

Finally, do not make the mistake of trying to keep people happy during this difficult time. For the most part, that's unrealistic. Far better for you to get them mentally prepared for the hard work and emotional strain that lie ahead.

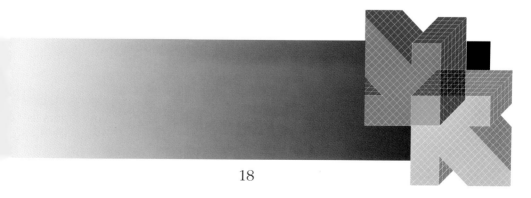

Provide leadership instead of playing politics.

Too many mergers get off to a terrible start because political issues contaminate the integration plan. The delicate process of *deal-making*, so appropriate and necessary in consummating the merger, spills over into the *management* process of combining the two companies. Courtship gets confused with leadership.

The problem lies in the fact that the moves involved in swinging a deal are very different from the management steps required to make the deal work.

Phase one of a merger involves analysis and pure negotiation. That stage ends as soon as the papers are signed and the deal is approved. At that precise point, phase two begins, and it's an altogether different drill. You immediately move into the integration management exercise. These two stages are as different from one another as catching a fish is different from cleaning and cooking it. And, to extend that analogy, many of the executives fishing for deals make a real mess when they get into the integration kitchen.

Some analysis continues in phase two, of course, and some degree of negotiation. But at this point in the merger the most precious skills are management and leadership.

Problem is, politics keeps getting in the way.

All too often the deal-making process is greased with flawed commitments. In an effort to facilitate negotiations, top executives play a little too fast and loose with promises, agreeing to the other side's requests or demands in order to help cut the deal. In phase two, these concessions come back to haunt the integration effort. Managing gets clumsy as people have to comply with the more awkward aspects of the agreement.

What's more inexcusable, though, is that the politically motivated moves continue, intruding into phase two unnecessarily and inappropriately. It's like management can't break the habit. Behavior that made sense in phase one now seriously interferes with proper integration methodology.

What does this look like at close range?

You'll see what we refer to as a "policy of appeasement" being played out. The people at the top, in particular, tiptoe around one another's egos, trying not to ruffle any executive feathers. Afraid they'll be accused of coming on too strong, management goes overboard trying not to antagonize anybody. Intent on staging things ever so carefully, they come off the line much too slowly. Valuable time slips away.

Mergers cry out for strong leadership and demand more management direction. But often the issue regarding who's really in charge remains blurred. Marching orders are either ambiguous or nonexistent. As a result, integration drags.

The parent company should be clear, crisp and quick in establishing authority. Because of misguided political sensitivities, however, merger management often bogs down in consensus building. While this activity wears on, power struggles heat up and people stake out their territories in ways guaranteed to cause trouble.

Even if it makes somebody bristle, you're much better off announcing immediately who's calling the shots. Say who reports to whom. Specify everybody's respective range of responsibilities. Be directive instead of worrying about bruising egos. Rest assured, this task isn't likely to get any easier later on.

Be willing to be unfair.

Mergers always require you to make sacrifices. It's a time of tradeoffs. Compromises. Less than perfect solutions. So far as the people issues are concerned, it's like watching a card game—some win, some lose, some break even.

You can care deeply—for everybody—but you can't keep from damaging some careers.

Deep inside managers know this is the case. Obviously, everybody can't come out on top. But when it comes down to deciding how the two work forces will actually be integrated, the people calling the shots usually feel compelled to make a show of fairness. Instinctively, they want to come across as acting equitably, to be seen as even-handed in the way they assign people to the various positions.

This sort of behavior is fully understandable. But as it turns out, it's not particularly good management. In fact, if being "fair" to current employees is a top priority, merging is probably a bad plan. It's sort of like wrestling with the decision of whether or not to declare war. How can you justify it if you're unwilling to sacrifice some lives? Nobody ever said that mergers are the kinder and gentler way to corporate growth.

All too often the attempt to be fair and equitable in the integration process produces bad business decisions. You'll see it at the very outset, where people are being tapped to serve on the various merger task forces and transition teams. Companies will bend over backward to get equal representation from both organizations. *Balance* is the big word. And it sells, because it suggests that people on both sides of the fence will have equal say-so on merger matters.

But should they? Usually not.

This approach emphasizes fairness at the expense of competence. And it's a flawed methodology because it implies that in the future, equal treatment is going to be the norm. That's not the message you should be sending these days. It's an *entitlement* message, suggesting that equality counts for more than competence. It implies that which company you come from is more important than your individual ability to contribute.

These mistakes show up most commonly in the so-called "merger of equals." But they occur any time the people in charge make staffing decisions designed to achieve *balance* rather than the *best*. Good management gets sacrificed on the altar of compromise.

This is the "one for me, one for you" fallacy. You get a V.P. of Marketing, we get a V.P. of Sales. You get to keep the fabrication plant in New York, we get to keep our regional headquarters in Texas. None of these negotiated "tradeoffs" make sense on their own merits, but somehow they come to be seen as reasonable when taken together.

This is lousy leadership. Bad management. It takes "fairness" down to too local a level. Looked at in the broader scheme of things, how fair is it to stockholders? To customers? Even to the rest of the employees? Don't all those people deserve the best the combined company has to offer? What if this were two professional football teams being merged—would you go for fair representation from each team in your starting lineup, or would you field your very best talent?

Now is the time to go for organizational upgrades. Choose the best, regardless of which company provides it. Don't shoot for a 50-50 deal. Go for 70-30, or 10-90—whatever makes you stronger, faster, more competitive. Whether you're talking managers, facilities, product lines, sales teams, R & D projects, even brand names, be willing to be "unfair." Favor the best, instead of playing the game of politically correct tradeoffs.

Re-recruit your key people.

I f you're involved in a merger, some of your best people are job hunting. Count on it.

Maybe you don't have many who are circulating their resumes yet, but you can bet the majority are considering their options. Mergers are good at getting people's attention. Everybody wakes up, looks around, and wonders how his or her career will be affected.

Some people can't stand all the uncertainty and ambiguity, so they start looking for opportunities somewhere else. Others have a pretty good idea of what's coming, but don't like the looks of what they see. So they, too, decide to check out other job possibilities. The most talented people, of course, typically have the best alternatives. Executive recruiters aggressively seek them out, knowing that mergers always loosen the ties that bind.

Research shows that acquired firms, on the average, lose four out of ten managers during the first twenty-four months of a merger. This turnover rate is three times the rate found in companies that aren't involved in a merger. In hostile takeovers, the turnover rate among managers jumps above 50 percent. Nobody tracks the turnover statistics on other important personnel such as key technical talent, the best sales people, and so on, but there's no reason to believe their data would look very different.

Often, of course, people are the most precious part of the deal. If the top talent leaves, the value of the acquisition drops through the floor. That's bad enough. But what makes the problem even worse is that those who depart frequently join up with and strengthen your competitors.

You might as well operate from the premise that everybody, in both organizations, is considering other employment. With that as your mental framework, take a close look at the situation. Who will be most crucial to the success of the merger? Who can you not afford to lose?

Figure this out in a hurry, and engineer a re-recruitment effort that helps you hang onto these folks. Make it resemble a full court press.

What should re-recruitment look like? Well, it should be like basic recruitment, but even better. After all, you've got more invested in these people than you would in a newcomer. Some fundamentals—

- Make the target person feel special, not taken for granted.

- Keep the communication lines open and active.

- Take the person into your confidence, asking for his or her ideas and opinions.

- Try to give the individual a key role, a special assignment that makes it clear that he or she is a highly valued individual.

- Consider giving a raise, a higher ranking title, or a "stay" bonus.

Above all, don't assume people are planning to stick with you just because they're not talking about leaving. Most folks don't announce their intentions in a public fashion. In fact, if you don't start re-recruiting until a person seems visibly troubled or talks openly about leaving, you've probably waited too long. Chances are your high talent employee, though still on your payroll, has already moved in emotionally to a new job. The heart always leaves before the body.

Finally, you need to know that turnover peaks at two times in the typical merger scenario. The first vulnerable point is early on—during the first several weeks—when the integration process is just getting under way. This suggests you need to attack the situation immediately. The second exodus occurs some months later, as the new organization finally takes shape and people get an accurate sense of what it's going to be like to work in the merged organization. At this point the wait-and-see period is over. Now comes the second turnover surge, as some of the people who were patient enough to "give it a shot" decide the merger hasn't worked in their best interests. This crew is harder to re-recruit. The secret lies in starting early and being willing to invest as much time and effort as you would have to spend in attracting replacement personnel.

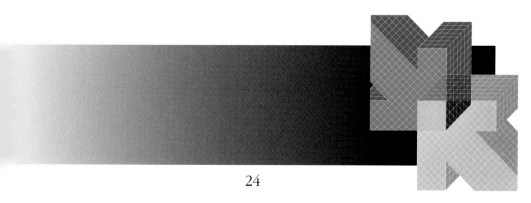

Instead of trying to stabilize the situation, exploit instability.

W hen it comes to categorizing organizational change, mergers stand as the seismic event. Nothing else even comes close. Not even bankruptcy.

Unlike piece-meal change, mergers have it all. Consolidation requires a restructuring of sorts. Redundancies lead to downsizing. Cultures clash. Systems and processes must be reworked and reconciled. Policies and procedures get revamped. The product line can double overnight. The whole power structure gets re-negotiated.

All this (and more) takes place simultaneously, and all in the white-hot glare of the public eye. Everybody's watching—Wall Street, shareholders, suppliers, customers, competitors, employees, and the media. How's that for real pressure?

Mergers shatter the status quo. Soon the entire organization seems off balance. Before long the destabilization begins to eat on people big time, and management worries that the place is going to overdose on change.

What do your instincts tell you to do?

The most common reaction from managers and executives is both wrong and rather fruitless. They feel compelled to stabilize things. Their natural tendency is to try and manage change into submission, to make the situation settle down. Managing, in their eyes, is about being in control, and these circumstances give them the feeling that they're losing their grip. So they try to muscle the merger toward stability.

But now is a time to respect your limits. This thing is bigger than you. For the time being, you're not going to be very successful at bringing stability to the organization. You can waste enormous amounts of energy seeking organizational homeostasis, when, in fact, the destabilization can be turned to your advantage.

During the early months of merger integration, about the best you can do is manage the blur—ride the waves, so to speak, instead of trying to be boss of the ocean. You can't avoid the rough water, so you might as well make the most of it. The ride may be wild and scary, but you sure can cover some miles.

Believe it or not, there is a blessing in all this. Several in fact. With things in such a state of flux, you have a window of opportunity during which you can do dramatic things. It's like having a license to make whole-sale changes, to take actions that are long overdue.

People are primed for it. The energy level is up. So pull the trigger. Don't squander this chance to do more than merely merge.

This major uptick in corporate metabolism is something you desperately need to sustain. Rather than being disturbed about it, you should nurture it. The organization needs it to compete. And as for the intense instability, you should use it to develop a higher tolerance for disorder on the part of your people. That, too, has become an essential survival skill in this world of high-velocity change.

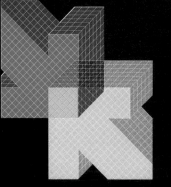

Fast growth is different

W hen it comes to growth, mergers are the fastest game in town. And you have to *manage* fast or you fail.

Of course, raw speed is not enough to guarantee success. Managing badly at high velocity is as big a mistake as moving slowly in hopes of avoiding error.

The secret is to move more rapidly—to accelerate hard—but to have the right touch at the wheel. Speed is *the* essential element in your management approach...it's just not enough by itself. You can't win the race against generic merger problems without it, but you also need to follow other fundamentals to keep from getting hurt in the fast lane.

This field manual offers a set of guidelines that gets you off to a good start...that increases your odds for merger success...that positions your organization for very special growth.

This much we know—all companies are not created equal. That's why they built a fast lane.

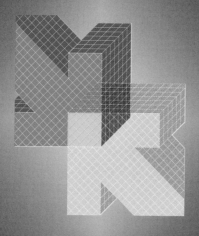

Management Consulting Services
from
PRITCHETT & ASSOCIATES, INC.

Pritchett & Associates consultants have the know-how to help:

- Exploit instability rather than merely cope with change.

- Assess your culture, organization, and management processes to develop high-impact change initiatives.

- Move you from plans to accomplishments...to become an adaptive organization.

- Apply leading edge change management expertise and merger integration services to your critical business challenges.

Please call
214-789-7999
for more information.

PRITCHETT & ASSOCIATES, INC.
13155 Noel Road • Suite 1600 • Dallas, Texas 75240

Senior Management Briefing
on
Merger Integration

This is a one-day session designed specifically for the senior management of companies planning or implementing a merger or acquisition.

The intense, high-level program positions organizations to:

- Manage the operational, organizational and cultural dynamics of mergers and their consequences.

- Avoid the pitfalls typically encountered during mergers.

- Recognize the risk factors and the "seven deadly sins" of merger integration.

- Develop a merger management plan.

- Establish a merger integration project infrastructure.

- Design a comprehensive merger integration communication strategy.

This program is a powerful first step toward developing the coherent integration strategy and senior management alignment your organization needs for merger success.

For more details, call our Pritchett & Associates consultants at
214-789-7999

The Most Practical, Solid, Well-Rounded Training in Business.

Training built on best sellers.

Pritchett & Associates' handbooks—used by more than 25,000 organizations and over 3,000,000 employees—are the basis of our training programs. Our intensive training sessions provide participants with the opportunity to apply the hard-hitting principles presented in the handbooks.

A high-velocity approach for maximum impact.

Our training programs are quick-impact and concentrated. They give your people a no-nonsense message on how to deal with today's rapidly changing business environment.

From top management to the front lines.

Pritchett & Associates has been consulting to top executives in major organizations for more than two decades. Our training programs are based on principles that cut across all levels of your organization to unify your people and get them moving in the same direction.

Results you can take to the bank.

Pritchett training is an investment that will yield dollars-and-cents returns. Our training focuses on a key source of profitability and productivity—people.

Training from Pritchett & Associates, Inc., makes the difference And that's the real bottom line.

Call **1-800-622-8989** for more information.

Order Form

Mergers
Growth in the Fast Lane

1-99 copies	_____ copies at 5.95 each
100-999 copies	_____ copies at 5.75 each
1,000-4,999 copies	_____ copies at 5.50 each
5,000-9,999 copies	_____ copies at 5.25 each
10,000 or more copies	_____ copies at 5.00 each

To place orders, call toll free **800-992-5922**
or drop your order in the mail using this order form.
Orders may be faxed to **214-789-7900**.

Name _____

Job Title _____

Organization _____

Phone _____

Street Address _____ Zip _____

P.O. Box _____ Zip _____

City, State _____

Country _____

Purchase order number (if applicable) _____

Applicable sales tax, shipping and handling charges will be added. Prices subject to change.

Orders less than $100 require prepayment. $100 or more may be invoiced.

☐ Check Enclosed ☐ Please Invoice

☐ **VISA** ☐ **MasterCard** ☐ **AMERICAN EXPRESS**

Account Number _____ Expiration Date _____

Signature _____

800-992-5922
Overnight or Second Day Deliveries Available
via Federal Express or UPS.

PRITCHETT & ASSOCIATES, INC.
13155 Noel Road, Suite 1600, Dallas, Texas 75240
214-789-7999 • FAX 214-789-7900

95052

Other Books by Pritchett & Associates, Inc.

* Training programs also available. Please call 1-800-622-8989 for more information. Call 214-789-7999 for information regarding international rights and translations.

About the Authors

Price Pritchett is Chairman and CEO of Pritchett & Associates, Inc., a Dallas-based firm specializing in merger integration strategy and organizational change. He has authored 17 books, and is recognized internationally as a leading authority on merger dynamics and change management. He holds a Ph.D. in psychology and has consulted to top executives in major corporations for two decades.

Robert D. Gilbreath is Vice President of Consulting for Pritchett & Associates. He is the author of six previous books, including *Escape from Management Hell* and *Save Yourself!*, and has led major corporate transformations and merger integration efforts on six continents. A distinguished lecturer at leading universities worldwide, Bob has addressed hundreds of groups and been a regular commentator on national and international radio and television networks.

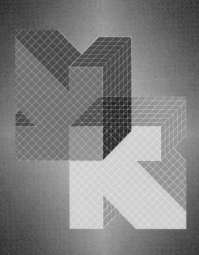